When the Sun Goes Dark

Andrew Fraknoi

Dennis Schatz

Illustrated by Eric Freeberg

NSTA Kids
National Science Teachers Association

Arlington, Virginia

National Science Teachers Association

Claire Reinburg, Director
Wendy Rubin, Managing Editor
Rachel Ledbetter, Associate Editor
Amanda Van Beuren, Associate Editor
Donna Yudkin, Book Acquisitions Coordinator

ART AND DESIGN
Will Thomas Jr., Director
Joseph Butera, Senior Graphic Designer, Cover and Interior Design
Illustrated by Eric Freeberg

PRINTING AND PRODUCTION
Catherine Lorrain, Director

NATIONAL SCIENCE TEACHERS ASSOCIATION
David L. Evans, Executive Director
David Beacom, Publisher

1840 Wilson Blvd., Arlington, VA 22201
www.nsta.org/store
For customer service inquiries, please call 800-277-5300.

Lexile® measure: 890L

NSTA is committed to publishing material that promotes the best in inquiry-based science education. However, conditions of actual use may vary, and the safety procedures and practices described in this book are intended to serve only as a guide. Additional precautionary measures may be required. NSTA and the authors do not warrant or represent that the procedures and practices in this book meet any safety code or standard of federal, state, or local regulations. NSTA and the authors disclaim any liability for personal injury or damage to property arising out of or relating to the use of this book, including any of the recommendations, instructions, or materials contained therein.

Library of Congress Cataloging-in-Publication Data

Names: Fraknoi, Andrew. | Schatz, Dennis.
Title: When the sun goes dark / by Andrew Fraknoi and Dennis Schatz.
Description: Arlington, VA : National Science Teachers Association, [2017] |
   Audience: Age 10-14.
Identifiers: LCCN 2016024881 (print) | LCCN 2016025040 (ebook) |
   ISBN 9781681400112 (print) | ISBN 9781681400129 (e-book)

   Subjects: LCSH: Solar eclipses--Juvenile literature.

Classification: LCC QB541.5 .F73 2016 (print) | LCC QB541.5 (ebook) | DDC
   523.7/8--dc23

LC record available at https://lccn.loc.gov/2016024881

This book is dedicated to our children,
Alex, Colin, and Evan.

The doorbell rang, and there were my grandparents. They had come straight from the airport to be on time for my 12th birthday celebration. They had goosebumps, though, because they were wearing only summer shirts and pants, no jackets. Grandma had a big camera case around her neck that she had to take off before she could give me one of her supersize hugs.

"Hello, Diana," she said, "and happy birthday." Then she gave my little brother, Sammy, a hug, too.

During dinner, Grandma and Grandpa told us about their latest adventures. I knew they traveled a lot, but this trip seemed more complicated than usual. It included two long plane flights that took almost a whole day, and then a boat ride to get to a little island in the Pacific Ocean—all so they could see something that lasted only five minutes.

But that something made the Sun disappear in the middle of the day!

Grandma was telling us about the big event during their trip. First, the Sun looked like it had a little bite taken out of it. They had to use special glasses to be able to look at the Sun without hurting their eyes. Then that dark bite out of the Sun got bigger and bigger. When the Sun was almost covered, it looked like a diamond ring for a second. After that, not only the Sun but also the sky turned dark. The birds even stopped singing. The stars came out in the middle of the day. All of the people watching with my grandparents oohed and aahed because there was a halo of light around the Sun that was very beautiful.

"The darkness only lasted four or five minutes," Grandma said.

Then everything that had happened before went backward. They quickly needed their glasses again because more and more of the bright Sun became visible. They could see the bite taken out of the Sun again, but now it got smaller and smaller until the whole Sun was back.

Grandma called the event a solar *e-clips*. I've heard of e-mail and e-books, but I didn't know what an *e-clips* was. But I didn't want to look ignorant in front of my pesky little brother, so I didn't say anything.

After dinner, I sat next to Grandma on the couch in the living room and asked her to tell me more about solar *e-clips* and what they were. She chuckled at the way I said *e-clips*, emphasizing the *e*.

She told me, "Most people say *eclipse* with the emphasis on the *clipse* part of the word."

So now I knew how to pronounce it, but I still didn't know what caused an eclipse or why people traveled thousands of miles to see one.

Earth

Moon

Sun

Grandma smiled and said, "It isn't hard to explain an eclipse like the one we saw. It happens when the Moon passes in front of the Sun, blocking the light from it."

Grandma could tell from the expression on my face that this wasn't clear enough for me. Then, she got that look she has when a good idea comes into her head.

"Let's make this room more like outer space," she said, "and then I can show you what happens with the Moon and the Sun."

She turned off the lights in our living room except for one lamp on the table. At this point, Sammy, who's always getting into my business, came in to see what was happening. Grandma told him he was welcome to join us in outer space. That hooked him; Sammy is really into space video games!

Grandma took the shade off the lamp, saying, "Let's pretend the bulb is the Sun, and Diana and Sammy, each of your heads is the Earth."

When Sammy, who has really short hair, said,

"Diana's head has too much hair; my head's a better Earth," Grandma just put a finger to her lips and said, "Sammy, it's quiet in space." I have to remember that line!

She gave each of us a tennis ball from her luggage and said it would be the Moon. She asked us what the Moon went around, and we both knew that it went around the Earth, although I said it first. Grandma told us to hold the tennis ball Moon with an outstretched arm and make it go around Earth (meaning our heads).

She then told us to look at the tennis ball Moon as we moved it around. When we held it in the direction of the lamp, she told us to stop. She asked us what the side of the ball facing each of our heads looked like. We both said it was dark.

"This dark Moon is called the *new Moon*," she told us.

I didn't think that was such a great name. Dark Moon would be better—but let's face it, we kids don't get to vote on things like that!

Now Grandma told us to move the balls around our heads a little bit at a time, going from right to left. As I slowly took the ball around, the side facing me started getting lit up a bit by the lamp's light.

Grandma told us to stop moving the tennis balls for a minute, then said, "That's what happens to the Moon. As it goes around the Earth, we see different amounts of sunlight reflecting off its surface."

As I moved the tennis ball Moon farther around my head, the ball showed more and more light. When the ball was on the opposite side of my head from the lamp, I held it high and could see it all lit up.

"What do we call it when the lit-up side of the Moon is facing the Earth?" Grandma asked.

Sammy didn't know, but after I thought about it for a minute, I thought I knew. "Is that a full Moon?" I asked.

Grandma gave me a thumbs-up, but out of a corner of my eye, I could see Sammy sticking his tongue out at me. He didn't like it when I got an answer faster than he did. But it's not my fault I'm older.

Grandma told us that the time it took for the Moon to go from new Moon to full Moon and back to new Moon is close to what we call a month. I was used to connecting months to events on Earth, like vacations, but I thought it was OK for months to be connected to something in space, too.

We moved the balls around our heads and saw different portions of the Moon lit up in different

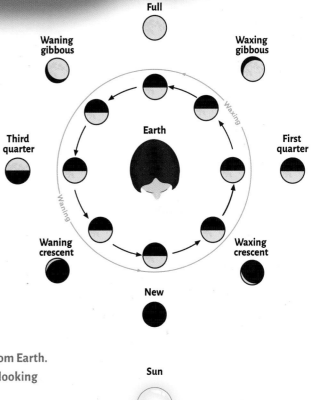

locations. In two places, the Moon was half lit up and half dark; in other places, we just saw a sliver of light, which Grandma called a *crescent Moon*.

After Sammy and I had explored for a while, Grandma said, "The different portions of the Moon lit up by reflected sunlight are called the *phases* of the Moon."

That was a good new word to know, but even after Sammy and I had taken the tennis ball Moon around the Earth about five times, I still wasn't sure how this was connected to eclipses.

RIGHT: The outer circle of Moon diagrams shows what is visible in the sky from Earth. The inner circle of Moon diagrams shows what would be visible from space, looking down from above the Earth–Moon system.

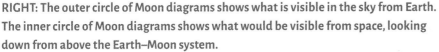

Full

Waning gibbous

Waxing gibbous

Earth

Waxing

Third quarter

First quarter

Waning

Waning crescent

Waxing crescent

New

Sun

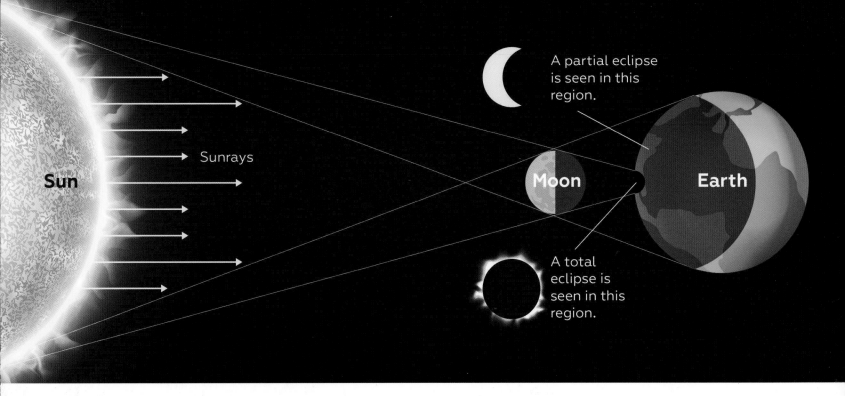

Sun

Sunrays

A partial eclipse is seen in this region.

Moon

Earth

A total eclipse is seen in this region.

"Well," Grandma said, "now you both know how the Moon's light changes over the course of a month. So let's see how we can get an eclipse.

"An eclipse of the Sun happens," she continued, "when the Moon moves in front of the Sun, as seen from Earth. For this to take place, the Earth, the Moon, and the Sun have to be exactly lined up."

She asked us to show her this with our tennis ball Moon. It took me a minute, but I finally lined up the tennis ball so it was exactly between my head and the lamp. If I held the ball right in front of the lightbulb, I could block its light from getting to my eye. An eclipse! I tried it a couple of times before I showed Grandma.

"Good job!" she said, smiling at me.

Sammy got it soon, too; he can be pretty smart, for a little kid.

Grandma asked us what phase the Moon was in when it eclipsed the Sun. I checked by looking at the tennis ball, and the dark side was facing me, so I knew it was a new Moon. Grandma had

to work with Sammy to show him how to see this, so I had some time to make the tennis ball Moon go around and around my head. I could get the eclipse to happen once during each orbit, when everything was lined up right.

This made me ask Grandma, "What makes an eclipse so special if it happens every time the Moon goes around the Earth?"

Grandpa was sitting on the couch the whole time. I thought he was asleep, but he was just listening with his eyes closed. When I asked my question, he whispered an idea to Grandma. I noticed that Grandpa often asked Grandma if something was OK to do; I liked that he did that. I think grandmas should be in charge of more of the world.

Grandpa then told me to get two of the Hula-Hoops he knew I kept in my room. I brought out a purple hoop and a yellow hoop from my collection and wondered what he was going to do with them.

Grandpa held the purple Hula-Hoop around his head and told us to think of it as the "moonthly" orbit of the Moon around the Earth. Sammy cracked up when Grandpa said *moonthly*.

"I know it sounds funny," Grandpa told Sammy, "but saying *moonthly* instead of *monthly* once in a while helps me remember that the word *month* comes from the word *moon*, because a month is how long the phases of the Moon take to repeat."

Grandma added, "If you count from one full Moon to the next full Moon, you'll count just about thirty days—or one moonth."

Sammy giggled, but I thought it was pretty cool to know where a word we use all the time comes from.

Grandpa then put the yellow Hula-Hoop around his head. "Now let's think of this Hula-Hoop as the circle the Sun makes in our sky during a year." I must have looked at him funny, because he stopped and said, "Diana, you look confused."

At first, I didn't know what to say. But I thought about the Sun and what I know about it, and I finally said, "Grandpa, I don't think the Sun circles around *us* each year. I'm pretty sure it's the Earth that goes around the Sun once a year."

Grandpa smiled. "You're right, Diana. If we were seeing it from space, we would see the Earth going around the Sun. But we are seeing things while riding on the Earth. For us, the Sun appears to be the one moving."

"It's like when you are on a bus, and the bus is moving by the trees on the side of the road," Grandma added. "But when you're sitting on the bus looking out the window, it can look like the trees are what's moving. Have you seen that?"

I thought back to times when I was on the school bus and knew just what she was talking about. Even Sammy was nodding.

Grandpa continued, "The yearly movement of the Sun in our skies is not so easy to picture. Grandma and I have been thinking about the Sun and the Moon for so long, we forget how much there is to learn."

That made me feel better.

Grandma pointed to the paintings we have on the walls around the living room. "Maybe we can use these paintings to explain why the Sun appears to go around the Earth each year," she said.

Grandpa's eyes lit up. "What a good idea," he said, looking at the paintings. "Just like we pretended that the bulb was the Sun and your head was the Earth, let's imagine that the pictures on the walls are pictures of groups of stars around the sky. We call such star patterns *constellations*."

I had heard that word before, but Sammy hadn't, so it was OK to explain it.

Grandpa moved the table with the lamp on it into the middle of the room. "So, Diana and Sammy, since your heads are the Earth, why don't you walk around the Sun and see what happens as a year goes by. Start here by me. What picture is the Sun in front of right now?"

We looked and saw that the bulb was right in front of the picture of flowers in a vase. Then we moved around the bulb a little and looked again. Now the bulb was in front of a picture of a boat with soldiers in it. As we "Earths" circled the "Sun," I saw that the Sun was moving around the walls of the room.

Grandpa said, "It's the same for us as the Earth goes around the Sun. On Earth, we see the Sun moving through different constellations during the year."

I got it then. From my point of view, as I went around the bulb, it looked like the bulb was going around the room. So as we watch from Earth, the Sun seems to make a circle in the sky as the year goes by. Now I understood what Grandpa was using the yellow Hula-Hoop to show.

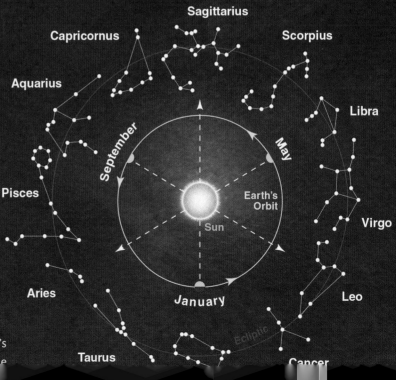

RIGHT: The circle with the names of the months on it is the Earth's orbit around the Sun. The diagram shows which constellations the

North celestial pole

Moon's orbit

5°

Ecliptic

Moon

Sun

Next, Grandpa did this odd thing where he held both hoops around his head at the same time, but they weren't lined up. The purple one was above the yellow one on one side and below it on the other side, and they only touched in two places.

Grandpa told us that's what happens with the paths of the real Moon and Sun in the sky. The Moon is usually above or below the Sun by a small amount. If they are not lined up exactly, the Moon can't pass directly in front of the Sun, and there won't be an eclipse.

"How often do the Hula-Hoops cross?" Grandpa asked me and my brother.

We both said, "Twice" at the same time, which made all four of us laugh.

"What do you think happens when the Moon and Sun arrive together at one of the two places where the Hula-Hoops cross?" Grandpa asked us.

I thought, *Eclipses happen when the Sun, the Moon, and the Earth are lined up just right. The only place that lineup can happen is where the hoops cross.* So I said, "Eclipses," and Grandpa gave me a big smile.

Grandpa then told us, "It turns out that the Sun and the Moon arrive at the crossing points *together* only twice a year. So we have a kind of 'eclipse season' roughly every six months when eclipses of the Sun and the Moon happen somewhere on Earth."

I had to think about that. First of all, this was the first time Grandma or Grandpa had mentioned that the Moon could have eclipses, too. I wanted to ask more about that later. Also, two times a year still seemed like a lot of eclipses. So I asked Grandpa why they went on a long trip to see an eclipse of the Sun if they happen twice a year.

My question got a chuckle from both Grandpa and Grandma.

"That's a very smart question," Grandpa said. "To answer it, you need know about the three kinds of solar eclipses."

Grandma gave all of us Ping-Pong balls this time instead of tennis balls. "Let's use these smaller Ping-Pong ball Moons with the lightbulb Sun and make some eclipses happen. First, can you make an eclipse in which the Moon covers only part of the Sun?" Grandpa joined in the activity, but Sammy and I didn't even watch him, since we thought the answer was easy. Both

Sammy and I held the ball so we could still see part of the lamp's light. Grandma knelt behind us and then said, "Right, you've got it. That's called a *partial eclipse*."

"Partial eclipses are interesting," Grandma added, "but they are not spectacular like the eclipse Grandpa and I just saw. And they're dangerous to look at without protecting your eyes because, as you can see, the Sun is still bright while they happen."

That made sense, because even staring at part of the lightbulb hurt my eyes after a while. Sammy had to look away, too. His eyes are worse than mine. He has to wear glasses to read.

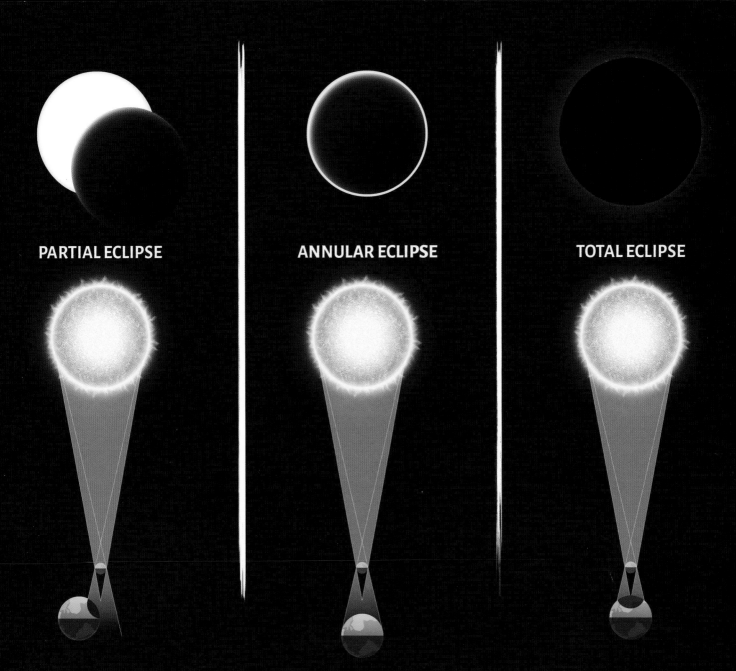

PARTIAL ECLIPSE   ANNULAR ECLIPSE   TOTAL ECLIPSE

Grandma asked, "Now, can you make an eclipse so that the Moon looks smaller than the Sun and a ring of light is around the Moon?"

I had to really stretch my arm so that the ball was still right in front of the lamp but didn't fully cover it. A ring of light showed around the ball. Grandma called that an *annular eclipse*.

Before I could ask, Grandpa added, "*Annular* is just a fancy word for ring. It's called that because you see the ring of light around the Moon. Those are prettier than partial ones, but they are still not the kind of eclipses we get excited about."

Then Grandma asked Sammy and me to make the kind of eclipse we had made before, where the ball covered the bulb completely.

"That," Grandma said, "is called a *total eclipse*."

"A little less than a third of all solar eclipses are total," Grandpa told us, "and that's the kind we like to go see because it's much more beautiful than partial and annular eclipses. It's one of the most spectacular sights in nature."

I like the word *spectacular*. But that still didn't explain why they had to go so far to see a total eclipse if every third eclipse is total.

"Let's talk about why we had to travel so far to see our eclipse," Grandpa said.

He held a Ping-Pong ball between Sammy's head and the bulb that was our Sun. The ball made a dark shadow on only one part of my brother's face.

"This is the same thing that happens on the Earth," Grandpa explained. "The dark eclipse shadow falls only on one small spot on the Earth at a time. You have to be right where the dark spot is to see a total eclipse."

I could see how there was one really dark spot on Sammy's face. Grandpa moved the Ping-Pong ball a little in orbit around Sammy's head, and the dark spot moved across his face. It went from his cheek to one of his ears.

"This is the same thing that happens to an eclipse spot on Earth as the Moon moves in orbit," Grandpa said. "The eclipse shadow moves along a narrow path that can be thousands of miles long before the eclipse is over. On the other hand, the shadow is only about a hundred miles across! You

have to be right in that path to see the total eclipse. Anyone outside it will see only a partial eclipse."

I had to think about those numbers. "How big is the Earth?" I asked Grandpa.

We looked it up on the web and I was surprised. The Earth sure is a big planet! If we put a measuring tape around the Earth's equator, the tape would be almost 40,000 kilometers long, which is about 25,000 miles. So only a small part of the Earth sees a total eclipse.

"So you see that each time there is a total eclipse, only people in the right location can see it," Grandpa said. "That's why people like us travel long distances to be where we can see a total solar eclipse."

I remembered that over dinner my grandparents told us they had planned this trip a couple years ago. So I started to wonder how they knew so far in advance when and where on Earth the total eclipse would be visible.

Grandpa turned the lights back on, and we got cozy on the couch.

"How did you know two years ago that this eclipse was going to happen and where you had to fly to see it?" I asked.

"Diana, when I got interested in eclipses, I learned that astronomers can predict them hundreds of years in advance," Grandpa replied. "It surprised me, too. An astronomer on one of our trips explained it to me like this: The movements of the Earth and the Moon may be complicated, but there are regular cycles to how they move. By *cycles*, we mean things that repeat regularly, like the cycle of the Moon's phases or the cycles of

the seasons from winter to summer and back to winter. Scientists have been following the Moon's and the Sun's cycles for many years."

Grandma jumped in. "A good example is the cycle of your birthday. Your birthday falls on the same date every year. But it's not always on the same day of the week, is it?"

"My birthday was on a Sunday this year," Sammy said.

"Exactly," Grandma said, smiling at him, "but it wasn't Sunday the year before. Eclipses repeat regularly, too, but where the eclipses are visible on Earth is not the same from one cycle to the next. Still, there is a pattern to them. Now imagine you

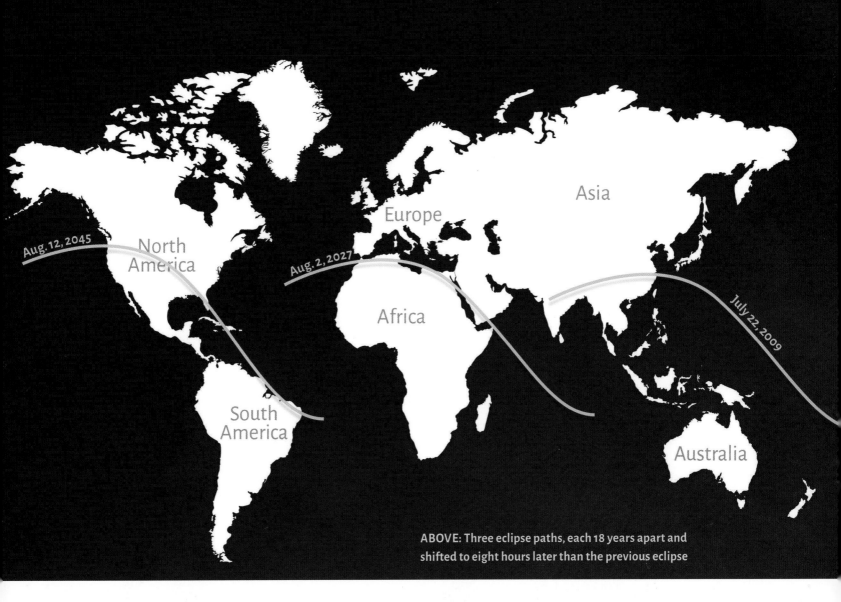

ABOVE: Three eclipse paths, each 18 years apart and shifted to eight hours later than the previous eclipse

have a friend whose birthday is February 29th. What would that be like?"

I was going to say that there is no February 29th; February has only 28 days. But then I remembered about leap years. We had just covered that in school. Every four years, there is a leap year, which means they add a leap day—the 29th of February. But I never thought about somebody actually having that for a birthday.

"Huh," I said. "That means the kid would have a birthday only during leap years. That's kind of weird."

"You see, some cycles take much longer to repeat than others," Grandma said.

"Astronomers discovered that eclipses repeat on an 18-year cycle," Grandpa told us. "So every 18 years, we get eclipses for which the exact lineup of the Earth, Moon, and Sun is the same. But the new cycle's eclipses happen eight hours later than the previous cycle's, so the path will be on a different part of the Earth."

I said, "Wow, that sounds complicated."

And Grandpa replied, "Yes, Diana, nature can be complicated, but isn't it great that people have been able to figure all of this out about eclipses?"

And I had to agree that it was.

The next morning, I went outside to walk our dog, Sirius. I looked at the Sun to see if part of it might be eclipsed. But it was so bright that it hurt my eyes, and I quickly looked away. At breakfast, I asked my grandparents about that.

"I tried to see if there might be a partial eclipse today, but it hurt to look at the Sun. How can people watch the Sun during an eclipse if it's so bright?"

Grandma looked at Grandpa and said, "We worried about this last night after you went to bed, Diana. We should have reminded you that it's always dangerous to look at the Sun without eye protection."

I smiled my best grown-up smile. "Don't worry. I know that, and I only looked for a second. But what do you do when you're waiting for an eclipse?"

"We're ready to show you in the backyard after breakfast," Grandpa said.

Grandpa had his camera tripod set up in the backyard, but his binoculars were attached to it, and one side was covered up with cardboard. I was moving to look through the binoculars, which were pointed toward the Sun, when Grandpa grabbed my arm and pulled me away. I quickly understood why when he said, "Diana, it's even

Sunspots

more dangerous to look at the Sun through binoculars! They make the Sun look brighter, so you can really damage your eyes."

Grandpa then showed us the safe way to see the Sun by holding a white piece of cardboard behind the binocular eyepiece. There on the cardboard was the Sun, nice and big and safe to look at. And when Sammy and I looked at it up close, we could see some black spots on the Sun's surface.

"What are those black spots?" Sammy asked. "Is the Sun's face dirty?"

Grandpa chuckled. "Sammy, that's not dirt! Those are called sunspots. They are slightly cooler areas on the Sun's hot surface that look black because they don't shine as brightly as the rest of the Sun."

Some of the spots looked bigger, and others were kind of small. I asked Grandpa how big the sunspots were and was surprised at his answer.

"Some of the spots are bigger than our whole planet," he said, "and the largest ones are bigger than 10 Earths put side by side."

Sammy and I said, "Wow!" at the same time. Then Grandma came over and said that she wanted to show us other ways to look at the Sun safely.

Grandma was facing away from the Sun with a large box on her head. Sammy said it was great for a Halloween costume, but Grandma told us it was a way to make a safe image of the Sun using a pinhole. Then she took the box off and showed us how it worked.

Grandma had an open umbrella near her feet, which seemed strange since it was a sunny day. But then she told us that she had put a small hole in one side of the umbrella, which produced an image of the Sun on the ground, just as the hole in her box produced an image of the Sun inside the box.

Grandpa then took some paper glasses out of his pocket. They looked like the ones we got when we went to see 3-D movies. He gave a pair to each of us and told us to put them on. I did, and everything went dark; I couldn't see anything. Then Grandma gently took me by the shoulders and turned me around, pushing my chin a little upward. Suddenly, I could see this ball of light through the glasses. I was looking at the Sun, and it didn't hurt a bit!

Grandpa told us that the glasses are made of a special kind of material that really cuts down the light and makes the Sun safe to look at. But he also said that we must check the glasses each time before we put them on to make sure there is no damage to them, and that they need to have a good, tight fit on our noses and behind our ears.

I asked him where he got the glasses from, and he said that companies that make special glasses

for movies also make them for eclipses. He ordered a whole bunch of them for his eclipse trips. He said that while the Moon is slowly covering the Sun, the glasses let him see what is happening. It is safe to take the glasses off only when the Moon has completely covered the Sun and the eclipse is total.

We sat on the grass and enjoyed a long look at the Sun. I even put glasses on Sirius in case he wanted to see what the Sun looked like.

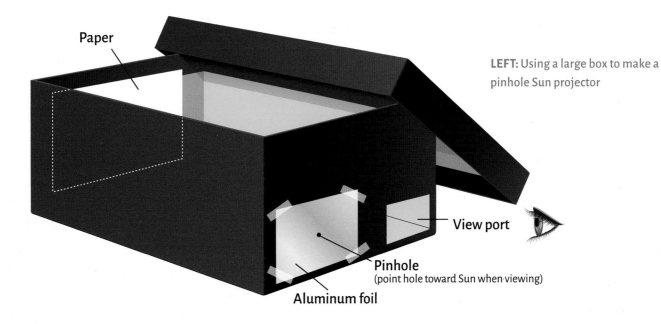

Paper

LEFT: Using a large box to make a pinhole Sun projector

View port

Pinhole
(point hole toward Sun when viewing)

Aluminum foil

Afterward, I was thinking more about eclipses. I wanted to ask my grandparents a question, but I had to make sure I said it right, so they wouldn't be insulted. I finally asked, "Are eclipses just pretty, or are they good for something, too?"

Grandma smiled and called me over to her computer. She said that she had asked that same question on their first eclipse trip, and one of the astronomers had given her a good answer. She wanted to show me some pictures while she explained.

Of course, as soon as I sat down next to her, Sammy was there, too. But at least he wasn't playing more video games, so I was OK with him joining us. Grandma showed us a picture of a total

eclipse, with a beautiful cloud of light around the dark Sun.

"This," she said, "is the atmosphere of the Sun. Just as the Earth has a thin layer of gas around it, so does the Sun. And we can see it only when the much brighter Sun is eclipsed."

She told us that the outermost layer of gas around the Sun is called its *corona*, and it was discovered hundreds of years ago during eclipses. For a long time, scientists could learn about the corona only during eclipses.

Then Grandma showed us some other pictures of the corona, and it was a different shape in each one. She told us that she took those pictures on different eclipse trips and that she was pretty

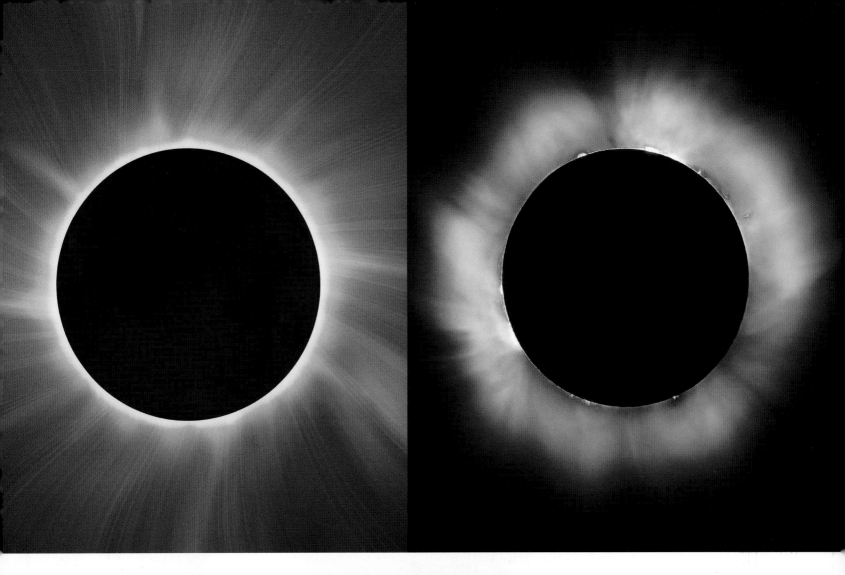

proud of how nicely they came out. I liked the idea that Grandma's pictures were part of the story.

"And here's my favorite part," Grandma continued. "Back in 1868, two scientists were examining the light of the corona during an eclipse. They have a way of telling from the light what elements are in the Sun. In the corona, they found evidence of a new element that had never been seen on Earth. One of them, Norman Lockyer, decided to call it helium because the Greek word for Sun is *helios*.

Norman Lockyer

Later, scientists found helium gas on Earth, too."

Grandpa said, "You kids may know about helium because we use it to blow up balloons for birthday parties. It's such a light gas that it floats in the air really well and helps balloons stay up."

Grandma finished the story by saying, "Quite a few other things about the Sun were discovered during eclipses, too. There are still astronomers who travel all over the world to observe eclipses, just like we eclipse chasers do."

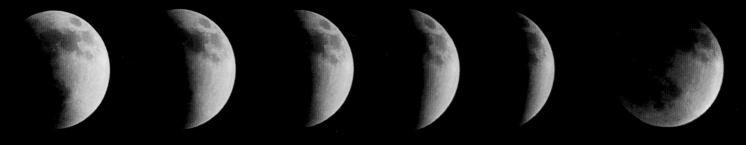

After dinner, I realized I had never asked my grandparents about the eclipses of the Moon they mentioned the night before. So I brought it up.

"That's easy enough to show you, because we can use the same setup—your head, a tennis ball, and a lightbulb—to see what causes lunar eclipses," Grandpa said.

"*Lunar* means having to do with the Moon," Grandma added, "since *luna* is another word for the Moon."

As Grandpa was getting out the materials in the living room, I thought about how we had used them before. Suddenly, I thought I knew what caused lunar eclipses. I was so excited that I ran over and picked up the tennis ball, then said, "I think I get it. I'll show you! Your heads will be the Earth again."

I turned on the light in the darkened room and told Grandpa and Sammy to have the tennis ball Moon orbit around their heads. I then asked them to put the tennis ball in the right direction to get a solar eclipse. Grandpa quickly put it in the new Moon position. My brother was slower, but he got it right, too.

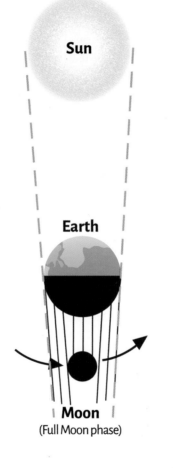

Sun

Earth

Moon
(Full Moon phase)

"Now move your tennis ball in orbit around your head until the sunlight falling on it is blocked by your head," I said.

They slowly moved the tennis ball around their heads. I could see that Grandpa was looking at my brother to see if he could find the right location without watching someone else do it. And Sammy did it—he found the place where the tennis ball went into the shadows of his head.

"Yes!" he shouted.

Grandma then asked what phase the Moon was in just before it was eclipsed. My brother thought for a while, then moved his tennis ball up and down to make it go in and out of his head's shadow.

Then he shouted, "Full Moon!"

He got so excited that he'd figured out the answer that he kept orbiting his tennis ball around his head, saying "Solar eclipse, lunar eclipse" each time it showed new Moon and then full Moon.

He finally had to sit down because he got so dizzy. I could then get a word in to ask my grandparents, "So, do people take trips to see a lunar eclipse, too?"

Grandpa called me over to take his tennis ball. He reminded us that during a solar eclipse, the shadow of the Moon only makes a small dark spot on the Earth, so not that many people can see the total eclipse of the Sun.

"Now," he said, "you guys are showing me the Moon just before it is eclipsed by Earth." He then asked us to look at each other's heads and tell him how many people we thought would get to see a total lunar eclipse.

First Sammy and I stared at each other with puzzled looks on our faces. But then I looked at the side of his head facing the tennis ball Moon. It was dark.

I thought, *When is it dark on the Earth? At night!* So I said (without shouting, because I'm more mature than my brother), "The Moon eclipse is visible to everyone on the nighttime side of the Earth."

"That's right," Grandpa said. "The Earth is much bigger than the Moon, so its shadow is bigger, too. It can cover the whole Moon. That means everyone on the night side of the Earth can see Earth's shadow on the Moon."

Grandma then showed us some pictures she had taken during a lunar eclipse. I noticed that the total eclipse of the Moon in these pictures was dark—not totally black, but reddish brown.

"Why is the Earth's shadow red?" I asked her.

"Good for you for noticing that, Diana," she said. "We get that color because the Earth has an atmosphere. The Sun is behind the Earth during the eclipse, remember? The solid Earth blocks the sunlight. But our atmosphere allows more of the

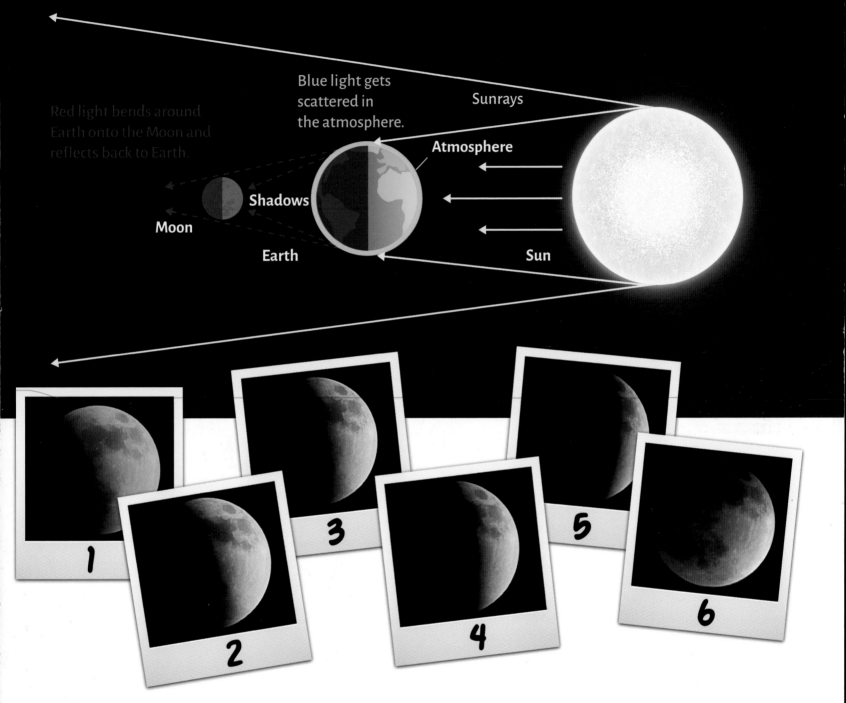

Red light bends around Earth onto the Moon and reflects back to Earth.

Blue light gets scattered in the atmosphere.

Sunrays

Atmosphere

Shadows

Moon

Earth

Sun

1

2

3

4

5

6

reds and oranges in the sunlight to get through and even bends the light into the Earth's shadow. We see that reddish light fall on the eclipsed Moon and color it."

Grandpa then told us, "A total lunar eclipse can last more than an hour, not just a few minutes like a total solar eclipse. Since it is already nighttime during a lunar eclipse, the change in light isn't so dramatic. And nothing new is visible like the corona becoming visible for the Sun. That's why we 'chase' solar eclipses and not lunar eclipses."

That made sense. I'm going to check out the next lunar eclipse on my side of the world. I also can't wait until Sammy and I are old enough to join my grandparents on a trip to see a total solar eclipse.

Glossary

Annular eclipse. An eclipse of the Sun during which the Moon looks smaller in the sky than the Sun, so that there is a ring of light around the dark Moon when the Moon covers the Sun.

Constellation. A pattern of stars that makes a connect-the-dots picture in the sky (like Orion the hunter). For astronomers, *constellation* has another meaning—one of 88 boxes into which the sky is divided, each named for an interesting star pattern inside.

Corona. The hot, dim outer atmosphere of the Sun, which becomes visible during eclipses.

Eclipse. When the Moon moves in front of the Sun (solar eclipse) or when the Earth's shadow falls on the Moon (lunar eclipse).

Eclipse path. All the places on Earth where an eclipse of the Sun is seen as a total eclipse.

Eclipse season. The time when the monthly orbit of the Moon and the yearly path of the Sun in our sky cross each other. During this time (which lasts from 31 to 37 days), eclipses occur. Eclipse seasons happen roughly every six months, and there are at least one solar eclipse and one lunar eclipse each season.

Full Moon. When the side of the Moon facing us is completely lit up (with reflected sunlight).

New Moon. When the side of the Moon facing us is completely dark, because the sunlit side of the Moon is facing away from the Earth.

Orbit. The movement of one object around another object in space. For example, the Moon has an orbit around the Earth.

Partial lunar eclipse. When only part of the Moon is covered by the Earth's shadow.

Partial solar eclipse. When the Moon covers only part of the Sun.

Phases of the Moon. Because the Moon reflects the light of the Sun, it looks different as it moves around us over the course of a month. Sometimes, the side facing us shows no light (new Moon), sometimes it shows a little light (crescent Moon), and sometimes it is completely lit by sunlight (full Moon).

Total lunar eclipse. When the Moon moves completely into the Earth's shadow, and the entire Moon goes dark.

Total solar eclipse. When the Moon completely covers the Sun in the sky.

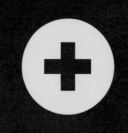

Additional Resources

See the special web page for this book at *www.nsta.org/sundark*.

Information for the 2017 total eclipse of the Sun (visible from the United States) is at *http://bit.ly/2bkGSvA*.

NASA Space Place
http://spaceplace.nasa.gov/eclipses

NASA's Eclipse Page for Grades 5–8
www.nasa.gov/audience/forstudents/5-8/features/nasa-knows/what-is-an-eclipse-58

MrEclipse.com—Solar Eclipses for Beginners
www.mreclipse.com/Special/SEprimer.html

MrEclipse.com—Lunar Eclipses for Beginners
www.mreclipse.com/Special/LEprimer.html

Suppliers of Eclipse Glasses

Many astronomy organizations, museums, planetariums, and telescope stores carry eclipse glasses. They are also available from these manufacturers:

American Paper Optics
www.eclipseglasses.com

Rainbow Symphony
www.rainbowsymphony.com/eclipse-glasses